life is
messy

this journal belongs to:

_____

_____

_____

life is messy

JOURNAL

BLUE SPARROW
North Palm Beach, Florida

MATTHEW KELLY

Copyright © 2020
KAKADU, LLC
PUBLISHED BY BLUE SPARROW

The-Best-Version-of-Yourself and 60 Second Wisdom
are registered trademarks.

All rights reserved.
No part of this book may be used or reproduced in any
manner whatsoever without permission except in the case of
brief quotations in critical articles or reviews.

For more information, visit:
www.BlueSparrowBooks.org
www.MatthewKelly.com

ISBN: 978-1-63582-236-6 (softcover)

Designed by Ashley Dias

10 9 8 7 6 5 4 3 2 1

FIRST EDITION

Printed in the United States of America

"There's no limit to how complicated things can get on account of one thing always leading to another."

- E.B. White, from *Charlotte's Web*

Contents

Introduction	1
The human dilemma.	6
A more beautiful question.	8
A more beautiful question.	10
Inadequate.	12
The worst year of my life.	14
What did I do wrong?	16
Unexpected.	18
When your reality becomes a nightmare.	20
Will the hurt ever stop?	22
Feelings.	24
Wait it out.	26
When nothing makes sense.	28
Dante's truth.	30
The dark night of the soul.	32

Emptiness.	34
Why is life so messy?	36
Have that conversation.	38
When evil comes to visit.	40
Life can change in a single moment.	42
Slow down.	44
The normalization of evil.	46
Dehumanization.	48
Closer than you think.	50
If I had a dollar for every time…	52
The great rehumanization.	54
Ambassadors of hope.	56
Thoughtless, careless, and reckless.	58
Mercy.	60
Future turmoil.	62
Life is difficult.	64
Turning to comfort.	66
Inspiration.	68
Cherish the ordinary.	70
Just for the joy of it.	72
Everyone is fighting a hard battle.	74
Beautiful kindness.	76
Roses and people.	78
Mourning the life that could have been.	80
The past.	82

Luck is a factor.	84
Getting unstuck.	86
Amazing.	88
A new path.	90
The mystery of you.	92
The forgotten obligation.	94
An intimate question.	96
Take an inventory.	98
Illusions and reality.	100
The most important conversation.	102
The way forward.	104
Move toward the light.	106
One choice at a time.	108
Three good reasons to do anything.	110
The four absolutes.	112
A personal philosophy.	114
The wisdom of simplicity.	116
How does life get so complicated?	118
Learn to say no.	120
The main threat to your wholeness.	122
A spiritual experience.	124
Three appointments.	126
Speak up.	128
A bad bargain.	130
Forgiveness.	132

Change something.	134
When change seems too daunting.	136
The basics.	138
Gently down the stream.	140
Becoming real.	142
Run toward yourself.	144
The guy in the glass.	146
Character is destiny.	148
Alignment issues.	150
Measuring your life.	152
Remember.	154
Peace, serenity, and tranquility.	156
The central question.	158
The mountaintop.	160
The good life.	162

Introduction.

Can someone who has been devastatingly broken be healed and become more beautiful and more loveable than ever before?

That is the central question of *Life Is Messy*. In the book, I wrote, "I am convinced that the answer to this question is yes. But as you will soon discover, arriving at this conviction was no easy feat. This book is my own messy and imperfect grappling with this question. If at any point in this book you find yourself lost, confused, or disoriented, return to this question. It is the North Star we are exploring. Whatever topic we are discussing in the pages ahead, though they are vast and varied, we will never be far from this question."

That is also the central question of the journey you are about to embark upon with this journal.

We need only change a few words in that passage for you to see exactly how this journal holds the potential to change your life.

Can someone who has been devastatingly broken be healed and become more beautiful and more loveable than ever before?

This journal can help you see that the answer to this question is yes. As you will soon discover, arriving at this conviction will be no easy feat. The journal in your hands will be your own messy and imperfect grappling with this question. If at any point you find yourself lost, confused, or disoriented, return to this question. It is the North Star we are exploring. Whatever topic we are discussing in the pages ahead, though they are vast and varied, we will never be far from this question.

I do not know how life has left you broken. But I do know that life leaves all of us broken in one way or another. Some of us are touched by trauma. Some are wounded by betrayal. Others are scarred by emotional or physical abuse. And still others are left with cracks and bruises over time by the inevitable difficulties of life. Grief, depression, violation of emotional boundaries, stifled dreams, divorce, isolation, loneliness... the list goes on because the messiness of life has many forms.

Whatever the nature of your particular mess, this journal is an invitation. It is an invitation to make peace with your mess. To cast off the pernicious delusion that your brokenness makes you irredeemable. And to find the bits of wisdom you need to start back down the path that leads to your flourishing.

Accepting that invitation may very well be the hardest

thing you ever do. I know personally just how excruciating it can be to face your mess and still choose to believe that healing is possible. But it's worth it. Because the choice to address your mess and believe in the possibility of healing is a prerequisite of human flourishing. You're flourishing. And you deserve to flourish. The world deserves to see the version of you that is vibrant, alive, hopeful and yet wiser because of the trials you've endured.

If even the idea of flourishing seems impossible to you right now, that's okay. Just know this: you don't have to get there all at once. In fact, you can't get there all at once. It is crucial not to allow the long road back to overwhelm you. Focus on taking the smallest step forward.

Lastly, I would like to encourage you to make this experience your own. This journal is not a manual for how to free yourself from the messiness of life. It's not a step-by-step process or a one-size-fits-all solution to heal brokenness. Any book that made those kinds of promises couldn't be trusted.

This journal is simply a vehicle to help you slow down in your life, collect bits of insight that will help you face your mess, and find within yourself the answers to some of the most important questions you will face on the path to flourishing.

To that end, in each section you will find just four things:
- A key passage from *Life Is Messy*
- A thought-provoking question related to the themes of the passage
- Space for your personal reflections
- A great quote to deepen your reflection and bring you encouragement

Spend time with the questions and passages that are most relevant to you. Feel free to move back and forth between sections, make connections, write in the margins... In other words, make it messy. Make it your own.

I suggest you date your answers to the questions. Not only will you be able to revisit them later and experience the questions more than once. But it will show you how God is moving powerfully in your life over time.

I truly believe this journal can serve you in the journey to make peace with your mess and find healing. And the best way it can do that is if you embrace it as your own. Facing your mess is deeply personal, but it's not selfish. Finding the healing you need and moving closer to flourishing is the best way you can serve others and the world.

I will close by returning to the passage that we began with. I left out the paragraph that immediately follows, but it will serve us more powerfully here:

Someone who has been broken and healed can become more beautiful and more loveable than ever before. That someone is you. My singular hope as you make your way through these pages is that you discover this to be true.

MATTHEW KELLY

The human dilemma.

Life is messy. You're not doing it wrong. Life isn't a color-within-the-lines exercise. It's a wild and outrageous invitation full of uncertain outcomes. Sometimes it is beautifully rational, at other times it lacks all logic. What appears to be a step back today, may turn out to be the first marvelous step forward ten years from now.

The mess of life is both inevitable and unexpected. It is filled with delightful mysteries and frustrating predicaments, indescribable joy and heart-wrenching suffering....

Acceptance is the only way to make peace with the mess. This acceptance will lead you to a profound acceptance of life, others, and self. It isn't surrender or defeat. It isn't conceding that there is nothing we can do about the mess. It's just a penetrating awareness that the meaning of life isn't to solve the mess. That's not the goal.

This radical acceptance of self, others, and life may be the beginning of wisdom. I'm not sure we can ever truly appreciate anyone or anything until we have made peace with the mess. Are you ready to make peace with the mess?

What is holding you back from facing the messiest parts of your life?

_____

_____

_____

_____

_____

_____

_____

_____

_____

_____

_____

_____

_____

_____

"God, grant me the serenity to accept the things I cannot change, courage to change the things I can, and wisdom to know the difference." - Reinhold Niebuhr (The Serenity Prayer)

A more beautiful question.

I am broken. Pretending otherwise is exhausting. But let me share with you the real problem with our brokenness. In our wasteful, consumption-addicted society, we throw broken things away. So, we don't know what to do with our broken selves. What do we do with broken people, broken relationships, broken institutions, broken families, and of course, our very own broken selves?

This is an important question, but a more beautiful question holds the answer. It is one of the most beautiful questions I have ever stumbled upon: Can something that has been broken be put back together in a way that makes it more beautiful than ever before?

Do you believe that something that has been broken can be put back together in a way that makes it more beautiful than ever before? Why or why not?

"It is in the confession of our brokenness that the real strength of new and everlasting life can be affirmed and made visible." - Henri Nouwen

A more beautiful question.

The Japanese have a beautiful artform called Kintsugi….

When a vase or bowl or cup is broken, artists gather up the broken pieces and glue them back together. Though it is how they put them back together that is steeped in wisdom and beauty. They mix gold dust with the glue. They don't try to hide the cracks. They own them, honor them, even accentuate them by making them golden. They celebrate the cracks as part of their story.

This is a beautiful lesson. They don't pretend the vase was never broken. They don't pretend that life is not messy. They don't pretend they are not broken. When we pretend to be someone other than who we are, our true self hides in fear and shame; the fear of being discovered and the shame of not being enough.

The most beautiful and surprising lesson the Kintsugi artform teaches us is this: We are each other's wounded healers. We each possess the gold dust needed to glue other people back together, making them more beautiful and loveable than ever. Our love, connection, acceptance, generosity, community, and kindness are that gold dust.

What do you possess that can be the gold dust needed to glue others back together?

___

"The meaning of life is to find your gift. The purpose of life is to give it away." - Pablo Picasso

Inadequate.

It's the possibilities that draw me forward. The possibility of love, community, greater meaning, connection with others, all the firsts and lasts of life, old friends, and new adventures.

What possibilities are drawing you forward in life?

"Start by doing what's necessary; then do what's possible; and suddenly you are doing the impossible." - Saint Francis of Assisi

The worst year of my life.

We are never ready for the storms of life. They rarely announce themselves. These storms come at unexpected times and in unexpected forms. They come in all shapes and sizes, and teach us that life is unpredictable and messy.

Think about the storms in your life.
What have they taught you?

"Hardships often prepare ordinary people for an extraordinary destiny." - C.S. Lewis

What did I do wrong?

One of life's enduring mysteries is that you don't have to do anything wrong for your life to go horribly wrong. When we are abused, rejected, hurt, betrayed, or manipulated, we search our hearts and minds, wondering what we did wrong. Maybe you did things to open or close doors, but it is not your fault.

What are you blaming yourself for that is not actually your fault that you need to release?

"You may not control all of the events that happen to you, but you can decide not to be reduced by them." - Maya Angelou

Unexpected.

We all end up living unexpected lives....

Life doesn't unfold according to our plans. But sooner or later, we each have to decide how we are going to make the most of our one, brief, unexpected life. It is then that we come face-to-face with two enduring truths: We cannot live without hope that things will change for the better, and we are not victims of our circumstances.

Hope is not always as accessible as we would like. It often seems just out of reach at those times when we are most in need of it, when our hearts are broken, our minds downtrodden, and our souls crushed. Yet, even in those moments, we have a choice. The unexpected is either a curse or an opportunity. We get to decide.

In what ways has your life turned out differently than you expected?
How would your life change if you treated the unexpected like an opportunity?

"It is strange, but true, that the most important turning points of life often come at the most unexpected times and in the most unexpected ways." - Napoleon Hill

When your reality becomes a nightmare.

Pain, trauma, and grief distort time. I would tell myself, "This is not a dream. It's not even a nightmare. This is my life." But that wasn't true. I would say to myself, "No. This is your life right now." And just adding those two words— *right now*—changes everything. It may be your life right now, but that doesn't mean it will be your life forever.

What pain, grief, or trauma are you dealing with right now? How can you remind yourself that it won't last forever?

"Let nothing perturb you, nothing frighten you. All things pass. God does not change. Patience achieves everything." - Saint Teresa of Ávila

Will the hurt ever stop?

Grief is your friend. It may not seem like it, but it's helping you heal. It's a mistake to pretend it isn't there. It is so easy to become embarrassed or ashamed of grief. This is also a mistake. Have no shame in your grief. Allow it to wash over you. Invite it to heal you. Just know that while there will be times when the enormity of your grief seems insurmountable, but you are more than your grief. Be gentle with yourself. Be patient with yourself.

In what areas of your life do you need to be more gentle or patient with yourself?

"Have patience with all things, but chiefly have patience with yourself. Do not lose courage in considering your own imperfections but instantly set about remedying them—every day begin the task anew." - Saint Francis de Sales

Feelings.

Feelings are visitors of the heart. Welcome them. Each feeling comes to teach you something very specific. Be hospitable to these guests. They are only passing through. Unless you ignore them. This detains them unnecessarily. You cannot get them to leave by ignoring them, avoiding them, or pretending they don't exist. They will stay until you attend to them. And when it comes time for them to leave, thank them for visiting.

What feelings do you need to attend to today?

"In order to move on, you must understand why you felt what you did and why you no longer need to feel it." - Mitch Albom

Wait it out.

There are some situations in life that need to be dealt with. They require action. There are other things in life that we simply need to wait out. This can be excruciatingly difficult. It is much easier to do something, anything, than it is to patiently do nothing.

Knowing when to act and when to wait something out begins simply by being aware that there are two options. Our instinct is to act; we have a bias toward action. This bias blinds us to every other possibility. We often don't even consider doing nothing as an option. Bold action is beautiful when action is what is needed. Any action is clumsy when what is needed is inaction.

Learning to wait things out is one of life's greatest lessons, and it can be learned only by waiting things out. Sometimes the wisest thing to do is nothing, it is also often the hardest thing to do.

What is a time in your life that was helped by patiently doing nothing?

"Patience is power. Patience is not an absence of action; rather it is 'timing,' it waits on the right time to act, for the right principles and in the right way." - Fulton Sheen

When nothing makes sense.

Life can be disorienting. It can happen quickly. And this disorientation can be brought on by either a positive or negative event. It can lead to a shift in priorities, but not always. Sometimes we repress our new discoveries about self and life. Disorientation is an invitation.

It's a mistake to focus on the negative. It's a mistake sometimes to think the bad stuff is all bad. It is often in the middle of nowhere, lost and confused, when nothing makes sense, that we find ourselves and come to know ourselves in new and brilliant ways.

Sometimes when your life has been turned upside down, after the dust settles, you discover that your life is finally right side up. Sometimes when you feel lost you are exactly where you need to be at that moment.

The question is: Can getting lost be a good thing? Do you view getting lost as inconvenient, frustrating, an adventure, or an opportunity? The answer is different for every person in every situation, but most of the time when we get lost, we don't even consider some of these options. Maybe getting lost is exactly what we need.

Can getting lost be a good thing? Do you view getting lost as inconvenient and frustrating or as an adventure and an opportunity?

"Not until we are lost do we begin to understand ourselves."
- Henry David Thoreau

Dante's truth.

When we find ourselves lost, we tend to think of it as a crisis. The reality is it can be a crisis or an opportunity. We get to decide. But this opportunity is not to be squandered. Immersed in these fires, we can learn more about ourselves in one year than any other ten years of our lives.

There is wisdom in the mess. Immerse yourself in the wisdom of the mess with all the courage and consciousness you can muster. How? Acknowledge that life is messy. Realize that we are all wounded and broken. Accept some level of responsibility for your mess. This acknowledgement, realization, and acceptance are the prerequisites for the wisdom of a messy life. Together they give birth to a piercing awareness of how we came to be where we are and what we need to do to continue our journey.

How can you immerse yourself in the wisdom of your mess?

"When written in Chinese, the word crisis is composed of two characters—one represents danger, and the other represents opportunity." - John F. Kennedy

The dark night of the soul.

The dark night of the soul annihilates anything you believe about yourself that is not true. Everything is stripped away except your essential self. Your old self is left behind and your new self emerges. And when the darkness lifts, you have clarity like never before, because all that is left is the self you cannot live without and a piercing sense of how to spend the rest of your life.

What are some things you believe about yourself that aren't true?

> "Clarity of mind means clarity of passion, too; this is why a great and clear mind loves ardently and sees distinctly what it loves." - Blaise Pascal

Emptiness.

We all experience emptiness, and we all have ways of dealing with it. I have dealt with emptiness throughout my life in a variety of ways. They have all been equally ineffective, except one.

I have tried to fill the void with work, pleasure, comfort, things, and plans for the future. But none of these bring satisfaction because these things don't rightfully belong in the void. When I am finished distracting myself with these things the emptiness is still there.

Learning to deal with our emptiness in a healthy way is one thing. Choosing to deal with emptiness in a healthy way requires self-awareness and courage. The difference between learning and choosing is akin to the difference between knowledge and wisdom.

I have only found one way that works. This is it. Find a quiet place, sit down, close your eyes, acknowledge God's presence, breathe deeply, talk to him briefly about how life has left you empty, and ask God to fill you.

How would your life be different if you tried asking God to fill your emptiness?

"Emptiness is only a disguise for an intimacy of God's, that God's silence, the eerie stillness, is filled by the Word without words, by Him who is above all names, by Him who is all in all. And his silence is telling us that He is here." - Karl Rahner

Why is life so messy?

Life should be lived with maximum intentionality. But too often we are conflicted and confused. When we act in these states, we usually cause pain and suffering to ourselves and others. Clarity is necessary to live with great intentionality. But finding that clarity is almost impossible in the midst of this crazy, noisy, busy world. That's why having time in silence and solitude each day is essential.

In what areas of your life are you living with maximum intentionality? In what areas are you searching for clarity?

_____
_____
_____
_____
_____
_____
_____
_____
_____
_____
_____
_____
_____
_____
_____

"Silence is God's first language." - Saint John of the Cross

Have that conversation.

There is a conversation that you need to have. You know it. You may be avoiding it. Whatever conversation you are most afraid to have is probably the conversion you need most right now.

What conversation are you avoiding right now?

"Avoiding problems you need to face is avoiding the life you need to live." - Paulo Coelho

When evil comes to visit.

It is popular these days to dismiss the idea of good and evil as the nonsense of another age. But evil exists. When forced to acknowledge the devastating reality of evil, our tendency is to think of it as something far away. Until one day you turn the corner and there it is, and your life will never be the same.

The sad and tragic truth is that evil is never far away.

Where have you seen evil in your life?

"To ignore evil is to become an accomplice to it."

- Martin Luther King, Jr.

Life can change in a single moment.

Life can change in a single moment. This is not just the stuff of movies and fairy tales. Your life really can change in an instant, for better or for worse.

Some life-changing moments lift up our hearts and make us feel like we are on top of the world, but others are soul-crushing.

Life can change in the blink of an eye, but most of the significant changes in our lives build over time before compounding into something wonderful or devastating.

How has your life been changed in a single moment?

"Change is inevitable. Growth is optional." - John C. Maxwell

Slow down.

Every step is part of life, and there is life in every step. Life isn't a race, it's a dance. Every step forward and every step back, stepping sidewards and twirling in circles, are all part of the dance we call life.

Great dancers are never in a hurry. They relax into the rhythm, become one with their partners, and experience the exhilaration of the dance. When was the last time your life felt like that?

Simply slowing down improves almost everything in our lives.

When was the last time your life felt like a dance? In what areas of life do you need to slow down?

"The purpose of life is to live it, to taste experience to the utmost, to reach out eagerly and without fear for newer and richer experience." - Eleanor Roosevelt

The normalization of evil.

Every age has new storytellers, but one truth endures: We become the stories we read, hear, and watch. Today's storytellers appear to be committed to the normalization of evil, and by extension the annihilation of human dignity. Not the dignity of some anonymous people, but the annihilation of your dignity, my dignity, and the dignity of our spouses, children, grandchildren, friends, colleagues, and neighbors. Evil is much closer than we suspect.

What stories are currently influencing your life? Who are the storytellers you listen to?

"The most deadly poison of our times is indifference. And this happens, although the praise of God should know no limits. Let us strive, therefore, to praise Him to the greatest extent of our powers." - Saint Maximilian Kolbe

Dehumanization.

When you dehumanize people, it changes the way they treat each other. People begin to debase each other, rather than ennobling each other. For example, brutality debases us, while love and respect ennoble us. Do we live in a society of love and respect or a society of brutality? The question itself is unsettling. The answer is not binary, but still, too much of our society is engaged in various forms of brutality to dismiss the question.

Do you live in a society of love and respect or a society of brutality?

"We must love our neighbor as being made in the image of God and as an object of His love." - Saint Vincent de Paul

Closer than you think.

Every day we participate in conversations that could easily turn into gossip if we are not careful. How do we know when a conversation crosses that line? We could put together a list that includes speaking negatively or maliciously about someone, making a person appear incompetent or adequate, making public what should be kept private, criticizing or lying about a person, and so on. It would be a long list. But gossip is one of those things, you know it when you see it.

It doesn't hurt to have a couple of quick litmus tests at the ready to gain clarity as situations are playing out. Will other people think less of the person you are speaking about if you say what you are about to say? Would you like someone else to say those things about you? Reason and motive are also powerful indicators. Why are you saying it? Do you have a valid reason for saying what you are saying? What is your motive for saying it?

How have you been damaged by gossip?
How have you damaged others with gossip?
How can you avoid participating in gossip
in the future?

"How much time he gains who does not look to see what his neighbor says or does or thinks, but only at what he does himself, to make it just and holy." - Marcus Aurelius

If I had a dollar for every time...

Social media has made it easier than ever to ruin a person's reputation. The damage you can do to a person via these platforms is almost limitless. This is especially true because the world of social media is uniquely unforgiving. Do you want to live in a world without forgiveness? A world without second chances and new beginnings? Do you want to live in a world where you don't even get a chance to admit that you were wrong and that you can do better? A world where you are just written off and dismissed? This is the world social media has created….

Exploring these questions can radically alter the role we allow it to play in our lives and in society.

Do you want to live in a world without forgiveness? How have you seen social media be unforgiving? How can you be more intentional in your relationship with social media?

"We prematurely write off people as failures. We are too much in awe of those who succeed and far too dismissive of those who fail." - Malcolm Gladwell

The great rehumanization.

The process of rehumanization reminds us what it means to be an individual of worth. It rekindles a healthy sense of personal identity and helps us rediscover our humanity.

Rehumanization is about learning to see ourselves and others as human again. It may sound ridiculous, but you would be amazed at how many ways we have been conditioned not to see ourselves as human beings. One of the most blatant and common examples is our inability to express our needs. To be human is to need, and yet, we have been conditioned to believe that it is not alright to need certain things.

In order to see and value the humanity of another person we have to be able to see and value our own humanity. Learning to accept that we are wounded and broken is essential to the process of rehumanization. Discovering your own brokenness and realizing that you can be put back together and healed to become more beautiful and more lovable than ever before is the summit of rehumanization.

Do you believe you are an individual of worth? How would your life change if you viewed every person as an individual of worth?

"Wholeness does not mean perfection: it means embracing brokenness as an integral part of life." - Parker J. Palmer

Ambassadors of hope.

There is a battle raging in each and every human heart. This battle is between hope and despair and we can tip the balance by embracing the call to become ambassadors of hope....

Our actions can tip the balance between hope and despair. That is a power that should be used often and respected always.

How can you tip the balance towards hope and away from despair in other people's hearts?
Are you an ambassador of hope?
If not, what is holding you back?

"Hope is being able to see that there is light despite all the darkness." - Desmond Tutu

Thoughtless, careless, and reckless.

The origin of recklessness is thoughtlessness. We have all been thoughtless, and we have all been the victims of other people's thoughtlessness. It stings but the pain doesn't linger for long. If we are thoughtless often enough, we become careless. If you have ever been on the receiving end of carelessness, you know it changes you. When people are careless with our safety, or careless with our trust, or careless with our hearts, it hurts. This pain is real.

Depending on how egregious the carelessness is we may never fully recover. It has the potential to make us cynical, jaded, untrusting, and miserable. But it changes most people in this way: We become more cautious with people, we are gentler with others, and we give them the benefit of the doubt, because we don't want to be on the giving end of carelessness.

How would your life change if you were more cautious and gentler with others, giving them the benefit of the doubt?

"Thoughtfulness is the beginning of great sanctity. If you learn this art of being thoughtful, you will become more and more Christ-like, for his heart was meek and he always thought of others. Our vocation, to be beautiful, must be full of thought for others." - Mother Teresa

Mercy.

We used to play a game called Mercy at school when I was child. Two players grasp each other's hands and interlock their fingers. Each player attempts to bend back his opponent's hand or twist their fingers until the opponent surrenders by crying out "Mercy!"

Sometimes I wish I could call mercy on life, and that doing so would relieve the pressure and the pain, not indefinitely, just long enough for me to catch my breath and recollect myself.

When in the past have you wished you could call mercy on life?

"If you feel "burnout" setting in, if you feel demoralized and exhausted, it is best, for the sake of everyone, to withdraw and restore yourself." - Dalai Lama

Future turmoil.

The future is uncertain but not completely unknown. There will be more storms in my life and yours. I know that. I just don't know when. There will be more turmoil ahead. I am sure of that, though I know not what disguise it will come wearing.

More people will lie to me, try to use and manipulate me for their own purposes, and more betrayal is never out of the question. Still, I refuse to lose faith in people. I refuse to lose sight of all the good. I have come to the realization that most of the suffering people cause, most of the atrocities they commit, are unconscious. "They know not what they do," was Jesus' assessment and I have witnessed this truth over and again. And yet, human beings are gloriously capable of love and kindness, and every manner of goodness. And it seems that when their survival is not threatened, if they have not been dehumanized, they much prefer goodness over all else.

How would your life change if you refused to lose faith in people?

"Never be afraid to trust an unknown future to a known God."

- Corrie Ten Boom

Life is difficult.

All our efforts to avoid the difficulties of life lead us away from everything that is deeply satisfying. If your goal was an easy life, would any of the following be possible? Meaningful relationships, deeply satisfying work, health and vitality, raising children, starting a business, or mastery of a profession or hobby?

What are you avoiding that you should be confronting?

When human beings are at their best, they face the difficulties of life head-on. They learn to delay gratification, embrace reality, release illusions, accept responsibility for their lives, and live in the wisdom that the most satisfying experiences are often difficult.

What are you avoiding that you should be confronting?

"Avoidance is the best short term strategy to escape conflict, and the best long-term strategy to ensure suffering."

- Brendon Burchard

Turning to comfort.

It is natural to turn to comfort during times of pain, distress, exhaustion, trauma, and suffering. Comfort has a role to play in our lives, but few things will test our wisdom and virtue more than discerning a right relationship with comfort...

The purpose of comfort is healing, rejuvenation, and renewal. It serves us by providing relief from pain and suffering, easing distress, and helping us transcend experiences. It prepares us to face the challenges and opportunities of life again.

But there is also a dark side to comfort. It is seductive and can easily become a way of life. When comfort becomes the goal of our lives, we begin a debilitating downward spiral. Once we are addicted to comfort, it shifts from strengthening us to weakening us.

Comfort is a beautiful servant, but an ugly master.

Just as life is not meant to be easy, it is not supposed to be comfortable. Be ever vigilant of the role you allow comfort to play in your life. Allow it to serve you in your trials and tribulations, and at the end of a long day of exertion, but do not become a lover of comfort.

What role has comfort played in your life?

"If the highest aim of a captain were to preserve his ship, he would keep it in port forever." - Thomas Aquinas

Inspiration.

Inspiration brings the best out of us. Inspiration plays a critical role in our lives. It can be the difference between feeling fully alive and the drudgery of slogging your way through another day.

What inspires you? Books? Movies? Comedy? Music? Nature? Prayer? People? Whatever it is, find a way to build it into your daily routine.

We thrive if we have a steady stream of inspiration. Many of us have never experienced that. We get a little bit here and there, from time to time, but a steady stream of inspiration is life changing.

How can you build a steady stream of inspiration into your daily life?

"Don't waste time waiting for inspiration. Begin, and inspiration will find you." - H. Jackson Brown, Jr.

Cherish the ordinary.

It was the ordinary things that saved me. I have experienced enough extraordinary to know that I would choose the ordinary over the extraordinary all day long. Learn to cherish the ordinary. Make a list of twenty ordinary things that bring you joy when you experience them consciously.

Allow the ordinary to heal you.

What are twenty ordinary things that bring you joy when you experience them consciously?

"One of the most important-and most neglected-elements in the beginning of the interior life is the ability to respond to reality, to see the value and the beauty in ordinary things, to come alive to the splendour that is all around us." - Thomas Merton

Just for the joy of it.

So much of what we do, we do out of obligation—real or imagined. So much of what we do, we do because we think we have to. We do so many things in our quest to be efficient.

What do you do just for the joy of it? When was the last time you did something just for the joy of it? It is one of the things I admire in people. Many of the people I admire do much of what they do just for the joy of it. There are things they do because they are obligated to, and things they do because they promised they would, and there are things they do simply because they are the right things to do. But they have more of these other things in their lives, more of the things they do just for the joy of it.

When was the last time you did something just for the joy of it?

"God made us for joy. God is joy, and the joy of living reflects the original joy that God felt in creating us." - Pope John Paul II

Everyone is fighting a hard battle.

People don't walk around with signs. But everyone's struggling with something. When we are mindful of this, we are gentler with others. When we forget this, we abandon our humanity.

Everyone you will ever meet is fighting a hard battle, even if it doesn't seem like it. We measure other people's lives by their blessings, but we don't see their hidden burdens. You never know what is going on inside somebody—and everyone has something going on inside them.

When we recognize that someone is fighting a hard battle, we tend to rise to the occasion. It brings out the best in us, and compassion and generosity begin to flow. So next time somebody is upsetting you, frustrating you, annoying you, or ignoring you, take a deep breath and remember that she is fighting her own hard battle. Allow the greatness of your humanity to rise up within you, and act with gentle compassion.

This was among the lessons I learned during this time of turmoil in my own life. It is a mistake to get completely absorbed in our own troubles. When we isolate ourselves, we don't cut ourselves off from the problems, we cut ourselves off from the solutions.

How can you help the greatness of your humanity rise within you?

_____
_____
_____
_____
_____
_____
_____
_____
_____
_____
_____
_____
_____
_____

"Our human compassion binds us the one to the other—not in pity or patronizingly, but as human beings who have learnt how to turn our common suffering into hope for the future." - Nelson Mandela

Beautiful kindness.

The more joy we bring to others, the more our own joy expands.

The greatness and beauty of the human spirit is undeniable in kindness. Kindness is beautiful, whether it is the thoughtfulness of a random act of kindness or the heroic kindness that involves great personal sacrifice. Examine the most devastating and disgusting moments in human history and you will find heroic kindness. The greatness of the human spirit often shines brightest when the world is darkest.

Kindness is one of the utterly beautiful expressions of our humanity. Everyday kindness, random acts of kindness, and heroic moments of kindness banish fear, soothe pain, revive hope, and restore our faith in humanity. There are times in our lives when we desperately need to feel the touch of kindness. And there are times when what we need more than anything else is to extend this beautiful kindness to another.

How has the power of kindness impacted your life?

"Kindness is the only service that will stand the storm of life and not wash out." - Abraham Lincoln

Roses and people.

There are three things I know about roses: They are beautiful. They all have thorns. I'd rather live in a world with roses than a world without roses. There are three things I know about people: They are beautiful. They all have thorns. I'd rather live in a world with people than a world without people.

Who is someone you are grateful for today?

"The optimist sees the rose and not its thorns; the pessimist stares at the thorns, oblivious to the rose." - Kahlil Gibran

Mourning the life that could have been.

In order to embrace the unexpected life, we need to mourn the life that could have been. Perhaps a dream didn't come true. Perhaps someone you loved died. Perhaps you were in an accident, deceived and manipulated by someone you trusted, or got your heart broken. Whatever the cause, the life you hoped and expected to live is gone now, and all that is left is the unexpected life...

Mourn the life that could have been if your dream had come true.... It is a prerequisite for discovering the exquisite possibilities that still lay ahead.

Have you mourned the life that could have been or do you still need to?

"An inconvenience is only an adventure wrongly considered; an adventure is an inconvenience rightly considered." - G.K. Chesterton

The past.

Don't fear the past. You are not what has happened to you. You are not what you have accomplished. You are not even who you are today, or who you have become so far. You are also who and what you are still capable of becoming. You are your realized and unrealized potential. God sees you and all your potential, and he aches to see you embrace your best, truest, highest self. He yearns to help you and to accompany you in that quest.

Don't let your past define you. It may be helpful to glance in the rearview mirror from time to time, but if you keep your gaze there for too long you will crash.

Allow the past to serve you. Don't let it rob you of your now. Don't let it steal your future. Delve into it occasionally to learn more about yourself, but avoid lingering there for too long. If you sense you may be lingering in the past in an unhealthy way, ask yourself, how is this serving me?

What event from the past do you need to ask, "How is this serving me?"

"Forgetting what is behind and reaching forward to what is ahead, I pursue as my goal the prize promised by God's heavenly call in Christ Jesus." - Philippians 3:13-14

Luck is a factor.

life is a mystery and there will be things we will never understand in this life. We can oversimplify them to satisfy our desire to know, but in doing so, we are only deceiving ourselves and creating illusions that will eventually need to be painfully dismantled. Or we can learn to enjoy mystery.

If we cannot learn to be comfortable with uncertainty, we cannot learn to live amidst the mess. Learning to live with not knowing is essential if we are to grow in wisdom.

How can you become comfortable embracing the mystery of your life today?

"In the courageous standing of uncertainty, faith shows most visibly it's dynamic character." - Paul Tillich

Getting unstuck.

When a car gets stuck in the mud, our instinct is to accelerate in a desperate attempt to set ourselves free. These attempts are futile. Mud flies everywhere, the car sinks deeper into the mud, and we end up with a bigger mess than we had to begin with.

We all get stuck from time to time. Sometimes we do it to ourselves, sometimes someone else does something to cause it, and sometimes circumstances conspire against us. And sometimes we get stuck because stuck is exactly where we need to be in order to pause and reflect on life.

It's okay to feel stuck. It's okay to be stuck. Just remember that you were not created to be stuck, you were created to grow. Rest a little, take some naps, cry a little, or a lot, but then listen to life pulsing through your body. You will hear that it is time, once again, to walk, to sing, to laugh, to dance, to live.

How would your life change if you used being stuck as a chance to pause and reflect on life before continuing forward?

"This is the key to life: the ability to reflect, the ability to know yourself, the ability to pause for a second before reacting automatically. If you can truly know yourself, you will begin the journey of transformation." - Deepak Chopra

Amazing.

Human flourishing. Isn't that what we really want? For ourselves, for our children, for our friends and spouse? And don't men and women of goodwill want this for everyone, even the people they don't know and will never meet? But what in society is set up with the specific aim of human flourishing? Does your primary relationship, your family, your social group, school, church, workplace, or neighborhood provide an environment that is uniquely nurturing? For too many people, the answer is no.

It's time to flourish. You can't do it alone. You need an environment that is uniquely supportive. That includes people, food, sleep, exercise, prayer, and reflection, feeding your mind with healthy ideas, and ridding your environment of toxicity. And don't forget: Everyone who really cares about you wants you to flourish.

When was the last time you felt that you were truly flourishing?

"Be who God meant you to be and you will set the world on fire."

- Saint Catherine of Siena

A new path.

It is so easy to sleepwalk through life. It is so easy to keep walking down the same street, so easy to keep falling into that same hole, and all too easy to adopt the posture of the victim and blame someone else.

Life may have you in a hole. Perhaps you did it to yourself. Perhaps someone else pushed you in. Maybe it just happened. It's time to get yourself out of that hole and find a new path.

How might God be calling you to walk down a new path in your life?

"Seek God's will in all you do and he will show you the path to take." - Proverbs 3:6

The mystery of you.

You experience everything through the mystery of self. Everything. Not some things or most things, everything! Your capacity to experience anything in life depends on how well you know yourself and how much you are flourishing.

When you are flourishing you have more energy, and the more energy you have the more your capacity for life expands. Yes, capacity for life. That's not a small thing. Lots of people are alive, but each person's capacity for life varies. There are many things that determine our capacity for life: education, emotional intelligence, supportive family and friends, and invigorating activities, to name a few. But primary to all these is energy. Your capacity for life literally expands or contracts according to how much energy you have on any given day and in any given moment.

In what ways can you increase your capacity for life?

"Energy and persistence conquer all things." - Benjamin Franklin

The forgotten obligation.

How you treat yourself is more crucial than how others treat you. If you are not willing to honor the marvelous creation God made you to be, you are unlikely to demand the respect you deserve from others. In order to thrive as a human being, you need to learn to put yourself first. Before you are a mother, father, husband, wife, brother, sister, son, daughter, boyfriend, girlfriend, neighbor, colleague, you are a person first. You are a unique and wonderful individual, first.

We put ourselves first by acknowledging our legitimate needs and tending to them, encouraging ourselves, silencing our inner critic, following our passions, taking care of our health, being mindful of our strengths and talents, and being gentle with ourselves.

We need to learn new ways of putting ourselves first that lead us to flourish. The world encourages us to put ourselves first in all the wrong ways. Each morning when you wake, remember your obligation to yourself. This is the forgotten obligation.

How well do you treat yourself?

"It's not selfish to love yourself, take care of yourself, and to make your happiness a priority. It's necessary." - Mandy Hale

An intimate question.

The darkest times in our lives have a way of bringing important questions to the surface. Pain and suffering demand our attention and can direct it toward areas of our lives that need adjusting. Pain asks questions, and so does suffering. There are some questions that deserve regular reflection, but the pressures of daily life often distract us. Some questions are more intimate than others, and the more intimate the question the more likely we are to avoid it. We can avoid life's biggest questions for a long time, but only at considerable cost to our progress, happiness, and spiritual health.

The question that life stirred up in my soul at this time was a most intimate one: Do you like who you are becoming? In the depths of my despair, I realized I didn't.

When you discover that you don't like the person you are becoming you have some soul-searching to do. It was time to go within. Yes, I had suffered some cruel, even horrific betrayals, but there is no excuse for allowing these events to change me the way I did. Our lives change from the inside out. It's easy to focus on the externals, but it's what's inside that matters most.

Do you like who you are becoming?
Why or why not?

"The big challenge is to become all that you have the possibility of becoming. You cannot believe what it does to the human spirit to maximize your human potential and stretch yourself to the limit." - Jim Rohn

Take an inventory.

A moral inventory is a written objective assessment of your life, including character defects, strengths and weaknesses, and a clear-eyed look at the hurt and damage you have caused throughout your life. It's a personal history of all our transgressions. It is a completely humbling experience that breaks down our illusions. Through it we face the things we don't want to remember, the things we don't want anyone to know about us, who we have hurt and why we hurt them.

Taking a moral inventory of our entire lives, and writing it down, forces us to face things about ourselves that we conveniently tuck away deep in the recesses of our hearts and minds. But if we leave them there, they fester into fears and resentments that poison everything in our lives, especially our relationships.

A personal inventory is also a unique way to develop self-awareness. It is a life-altering experience. If you really want to grow spiritually, set aside a few hours three Sundays in a row, and sit down and write a searching and fearless moral inventory of yourself.

How would your life change if you took
a moral inventory of your life?

"Mistakes are the portals of discovery." - James Joyce

Illusions and reality.

Reality will always seek to obliterate our illusions, but it is for our own sake. How we respond when confronted by reality often differentiates the sane from the insane, the thriving from the struggling, and the conscious from the unconscious.

If we refuse to let go of our illusions our future possibilities narrow. And of course, those most difficult to let go of are those that have lodged deep in our unconscious. These are the illusions that have become so naturally a part of us that to suggest we part with them at first feels like a suggestion that we cut off our own right leg.

To make the onward journey we have to gradually let go of our illusions and continually embrace a little more reality each day.

What illusions are you holding on to in your life?

"Sometimes people don't want to hear the truth because they don't want their illusions destroyed." - Friedrich Nietzsche

The most important conversation.

The most important conversation you have each day is with yourself. It regulates self-esteem and establishes your very sense of self. Harnessing this conversation to help you become the-best-version-of-yourself is critical. Allowing it to work against you, leads you down a long, slow, steady hill toward self-pity, mediocrity, and sadness.

How many beautiful, healthy women tell themselves they are fat? How many successful men tell themselves they are worthless? These illusions and dozens like them are so common they are clichés.

Choosing to spend time with people who build you up, accept you, and love you is a sign of emotional health and intelligence. But if we do not speak to ourselves in ways that are life-giving, we will not be able to receive the love, encouragement, and acceptance other people extend to us.

Be careful how you speak to yourself. Your words have power. You may never be quite able to fathom just how powerful they are. But don't waste this power. Use it wisely.

How can you use the power of your own words to lift yourself up today?

"The words you speak become the house you live in." - Hafez

The way forward.

life after you have failed, been disappointed, lost someone you love, been deceived, lost sight of who you are and what matters most, or suffered a devastating blow of the unexpected is like writer's block. You can ignore it, avoid it, pretend it isn't there, distract yourself in a million ways, but when you are done, it will still be there. The only way out of writer's block is to write, and the only way forward in life is to live. Just as a writer will do everything to avoid writing when she has writer's block, when we have been traumatized, we will do anything to avoid living. But life is for living.

What is one step forward you can take today that can shift the momentum of your life?

"Yesterday is not ours to recover, but tomorrow is ours to win or lose." - Lyndon B. Johnson

Move toward the light.

There are times when we cannot distinguish between the path forward and the path back. We have become emotionally and spiritually disoriented. At those times of debilitating disorientation, be still, catch your breath. If you sense it is time to move along, but still cannot discern which path to take, move toward the light.

Find your own way. There is no one path or recipe for everyone. You have unique hopes, dreams, fears, ambitions, talents, and needs. God will use each of these to call you along your own unique path, but always toward the light.

If you're not sure where you are or what direction you should be going: move toward the light. The light always leads us forward.

How would your life be different if you consistently moved towards the light?

"Look at how a single candle can both defy and define the darkness." - Anne Frank

One choice at a time.

Our ability to choose is one of the things that makes us uniquely human. However hopeless you may feel, get back in touch with your ability to choose. Remember, not all choices are equal. We celebrate free will as if the ability to choose guarantees a good outcome. It doesn't. Some choices complicate and some simplify. Some choices bring life, and others bring death. Some bring freedom; others slavery. Some choices breed hope, while others breed despair. Some choices foster health, and others foster disease. Learn to harness the power of choice, your choices, one choice at a time, for all that is good, true, kind, noble, right, just, thoughtful, and generous.

What is one choice you can make today that is good, true, kind, noble, right, just, thoughtful, and generous?

"Choices are the hinges of destiny." - Edwin Markham

Three good reasons to do anything.

The key to making good decisions is to choose what is good. It's not complicated. It's simple. Some people would say this is an over-simplification. But there is beauty, virtue, and peace of mind in choosing what is good. Thomas Aquinas believed there were three kinds of good worth pursuing: moral good; practical good; and delightful good. These may be the only three good reasons to do anything.

Reason #1: It is morally good. Examples: love, virtue, justice.

Reason #2: It is practically necessary. Examples: eating, sleeping, working to support your family.

Reason #3: It makes you happy.

What reasons do you have for making decisions?

"Do all the good you can and make as little fuss about it as possible." - Charles Dickens

The four absolutes.

How do you make decisions? What do you measure your actions against? The four absolutes are another way to consider what to do next. In the early 1900s, the Four Absolutes were developed to help people dealing with alcoholism get their lives back.

The Four Absolutes are:
1. Honesty. Is it true or is it false?
2. Unselfishness. How will this affect other people?
3. Purity. Is it right or is it wrong?
4. Love. Is it ugly or is it beautiful?

These are powerful guides. They provide startling clarity in a confusing world. They help us to examine our options before making a decision by helping us examine our motives. This awareness is essential to spiritual growth and any form of personal development.

What do you measure your actions against?

"Our only desire and our one choice should be this: I want and I choose what better leads to God's deepening life in me." - Saint Ignatius Loyola

A personal philosophy.

Do you have a personal philosophy? Without a personal philosophy, life can seem confusing and complex, because every time you have a decision to make, you need to build a philosophy from scratch.

This becomes exhausting, and decisions made when we are exhausted are rarely good ones. When we are tired, stressed, or in distress, a personal philosophy is especially helpful. These scenarios make it harder for the mind to reach decisions, because our clarity is compromised.

Become a lover of wisdom, a philosopher. This will help you become a great decision maker. Be able to look back on your life three months from now, a year from now, ten years from now and identify the wisest decisions you have made and the fruit they bore in your life. Make wisdom a priority in your life, and watch your life flourish.

What is your personal philosophy?

"Science is organized knowledge. Wisdom is organized life." - Immanuel Kant

The wisdom of simplicity.

Every day you face hundreds of choices, options, and decisions. We fall into complexity by default, and complexity has an unerring habit of creating a mess or adding to the mess. Allow yourself to be governed by a quest for simplicity. Most people don't. Not because this doesn't make sense, but because we don't spend enough time reflecting on life. We spend more time planning our annual vacation than we do considering our lives.

Adopt the wisdom of simplicity. You will never be sorry you did. Apply it to every aspect of your life. It is an excellent path to clarity and peace. The beautiful minds of every age have cherished simplicity. Follow their genius.

Simple living is the essence of wisdom. The desire for simplicity itself is a sign of wisdom. If you are stuck, the most natural way to get unstuck is to simplify your life, strip away everything that is not essential. To move forward you need clarity, and simplicity gives birth to clarity.

Think of an area of your life that you need to simplify. What is one step you can take to simplify it?

"In character, in manner, in style, in all things, the supreme excellence is simplicity." - Henry Wadsworth Longfellow

How does life get so complicated?

If you really want to embrace the simple life, you need to know how life gets so complicated in the first place. We complicate our lives unnecessarily in a thousand ways, chasing things we neither need nor really want. Swept along by a culture of expectations, most people never pause long enough to reflect upon the deepest desires of their hearts.

If we are going to celebrate simplicity, it's important to understand how our lives get complicated. We are not victims of complication. We run willingly into the arms of complication. We complicate life. Sometimes it is the result of one big decision and sometimes it is the result of a thousand little decisions. There are times when the unexpected events of life bring chaos and complexity, though it is usually their addition to the chaos and complexity we have already created that makes life stressful or even seemingly unbearable.

How would your life change if you allowed the wisdom of simplicity to guide your decisions?

"Deep and simple are far, far more important than shallow and complicated and fancy." - Fred Rogers

Learn to say no.

Work on being free to say no and your yes will be more focused, meaningful, and powerful than ever before. What you say yes to determines everything. And if you don't say no to the wrong things there will be no room in your life to say yes to the right things.

We say we want to live more meaningful lives, but we keep saying yes to meaningless things. Start saying no to meaningless things and allow a life of meaning and fulfillment to emerge within and around you.

What are you saying yes to in your life that you need to start saying no to?

"Half of the troubles of this life can be traced to saying yes too quickly and not saying no soon enough." - Josh Billings

The main threat to your wholeness.

The greatest threat to your happiness and wholeness is your unrecognized spiritual needs. You are a spiritual being. Life is not just a physical experience. It's clear that it is also an emotional experience, and an intellectual experience, but we neglect the reality that it is also a spiritual experience. We are obsessed with the physical aspect of self, while ignoring the spiritual aspect. You cannot live life to the fullest if you ignore your spiritual self. You cannot be fully alive without spirituality. You cannot thrive and flourish while letting your soul starve.

In what ways do you ignore your spiritual self? How can you feed your soul today?

*"Food for the body is not enough.
There must be food for the soul."* - Dorothy Day

A spiritual experience.

There is no substitute for a vibrant spiritual life. A rich inner life is essential to human flourishing. If we want to live life to the fullest, we need to give priority to the spiritual aspect of who we are.

"I am not a spiritual person," some people say. It's not true. It's a denial of reality, a delusion that will continue to clash with reality until alignment is reached. It's like saying there is no such thing as gravity.

I understand why many have rejected religion. I have met too many people with deep faith wounds not to understand. Still, rejecting something you need to thrive makes no sense. We are spiritual beings in need of spiritual sustenance. Feed your soul. Spiritual experiences are essential for your well-being. A spiritual outlook and a vibrant daily spirituality are crucial to the overall flourishing of each and every human being.

Have you ever had a spiritual experience?

*"We are not human beings having a spiritual experience.
We are spiritual beings having a human experience."*

- Pierre Teilhard de Chardin, S.J.

Three appointments.

When you come to the end of your life, when death is undeniably near, what will bring you unmitigated joy? Thinking about death is morbid some may say. I disagree. Far from being unhealthy, it is a valuable and meaningful exercise. Thinking too much about death can be morbid, but how much is too much? I suggest that you think about death only as much as is necessary to live life to the fullest.

When you come to the end of your life, when death is undeniably near, what will bring you unmitigated joy?

"The fear of death follows from the fear of life. A man who lives fully is prepared to die at any time." - Mark Twain

Speak up.

To need is to be profoundly human. We need. To think otherwise is to go beyond illusion and enter into delusion. We need air to breathe, water to drink, food to eat, to be touched and held, to love and be loved, opportunities to learn new things, and second chances. We need. To need is to be human, and life cannot be an amazing experience if you deny your humanity. This is the most tragic way we dehumanize ourselves.

So, speak up. You don't need to be obnoxious about it, but you will feel set free when you do. And the amazing thing is, the people who really love you want to hear what you have to say. They will be fascinated and enamored.

Are you afraid to admit your needs?

"Having needs is not evidence of weakness—it is human."

- Danielle Bernock

A bad bargain.

To get unstuck we have to stop making bad bargains. What's a bad bargain? When you lose more than you gain. I'm not saying the goal in life should be to always get more than you give. Lose is the word I used. Losing something is different than giving generously. And taking is something altogether different again. It's time to stop making bad bargains with yourself, others, and life.

Let's talk about the first and the worst. The first bad bargain we make is when we complicate our lives. When we complicate our lives, we always lose more than we gain.

The worst bad bargain you make is anytime you pretend you are someone other than your own wonderful self. If you have to be less than yourself for someone to like you, care about you, love you, or want to work with you—you are losing more than you are gaining and making a bad bargain.

Are you on the cusp of making another bad bargain?

"Always be a first rate version of yourself and not a second rate version of someone else." - Judy Garland

Forgiveness.

Whom do you need to forgive? It's okay if you are not there yet. Be patient with yourself. Just don't quit and allow your heart to become hardened. I know it's not easy, but there is no path forward without forgiveness.

And whomever you need to forgive, and whatever you need to forgive them for, is not worth preventing your onward journey. There is no future without forgiveness.

Whom do you need to forgive?

"Resentment is like drinking poison and waiting for the other person to die." - Saint Augustine

Change something.

Now it is your turn, and mine. Promise me you will change something. There is no need to be rash or impulsive, but promise me when you work out what it is you will flip that switch. This is a new springtime in your life. It's time for a new path. Have the courage to make the change, flip the switch, and you will look back a year from now with awe and amazement.

What will you change?

"They always say time changes things, but you actually have to change them yourself." - Andy Warhol

When change seems too daunting.

The messiness of life can be paralyzing. When we most need change, we often feel least capable of embracing the change we know we desperately need. But that's okay.

Imagine the smallest adjustment you could make to your life. Something tiny. So small it seems insignificant. Liken it to turning and facing in the right direction at the beginning of a journey of a thousand miles. That's right, not even the first step, just turning and facing in the right direction. If that's all you can manage right now, it's enough. Just don't let what you can't do interfere with what you can.

When change seems too daunting, just make a small adjustment, and pay attention to how your energy shifts and your spirits rise.

What kind of small adjustment can you make in your life today?

"The man who moves a mountain begins by carrying away small stones." - Confucius

The basics.

Imagine for a moment that you were injured in an accident and you had to learn to walk and talk again. It would be excruciating. Each half step, each syllable, requiring all your concentration and effort. And then, there is the mental anguish of not-knowing if you will ever walk again or talk again. Recovering from any trauma is like learning to walk again. It is slow and can be excruciatingly painful and difficult. Be patient with yourself. Be gentle with yourself. Celebrate every advance no matter how small.

What is one area of your life that you need to be more patient and gentle with yourself?

"Never discourage anyone who continually makes progress, no matter how slow." - Plato

Gently down the stream.

Row, row, row your boat
Gently down the stream
Merrily, merrily, merrily, merrily
Life is but a dream.

What thoughts cross your mind as you read the lyrics? Which words jump out at you as you read them? When did you last live a single day that reflects the wisdom of the rhyme?

"Nature does not hurry, yet everything is accomplished."

- Lao Tzu

Becoming real.

"What is REAL?" asked the Rabbit one day, when they were lying side by side near the nursery fender, before Nana came to tidy the room. "Does it mean having things that buzz inside you and a stick-out handle?"

"Real isn't how you are made," said the Skin Horse. "It's a thing that happens to you. When a child loves you for a long, long time, not just to play with, but REALLY loves you, then you become Real."

"Does it hurt?" asked the Rabbit.

"Sometimes," said the Skin Horse, for he was always truthful. "When you are Real you don't mind being hurt."

Perhaps all that has been happening to me, within me, has just been helping me to become real.

What does being real mean to you?
When was a time in your life that was difficult,
but helped you become real?

"Authenticity is a collection of choices that we have to make every day. It's about the choice to show up and be real. The choice to be honest. The choice to let our true selves be seen." - Brené Brown

Run toward yourself.

At the beginning of each day, stand in front of a mirror, look yourself directly in the eye, and listen to what the man or woman—in the mirror says to you. This will make you uncomfortable. But it works. Your eyes will tell you something every single day of your life if you listen.

What type of things will your eyes say? You know what you need to do. They are not listening to you. It's time for something new. Go for a walk today. You are a good person. Today is going to be a great day, try to enjoy it. You are not paying attention to your needs. You should go and see your doctor. This has to stop. Don't let them walk all over you like that. You need some time off. Your critics don't know you well enough to compliment you or criticize you. A true friend would never treat you that way. Call your mom. Do something to make someone else's day today.

Run toward yourself by listening to the man, or woman, in the mirror.

When you stand in front of a mirror and look yourself directly in the eye, what type of things will your eyes say to you?

"As soon as you trust yourself, you will know how to live."

- Johann Wolfgang Von Goethe

The guy in the glass.

The Guy in the Glass

When you get what you want in your struggle for self,
And the world makes you King for a day,
Then go to the mirror and look at yourself,
And see what that guy has to say.
For it isn't your Father, or Mother, or Wife,
Who judgement upon you must pass.
The feller whose verdict counts most in your life
Is the guy staring back from the glass.
He's the feller to please, never mind all the rest.
For he's with you clear up to the end,
And you've passed your most dangerous, difficult test
If the guy in the glass is your friend.
You may be like Jack Horner and "chisel" a plum,
And think you're a wonderful guy,
But the man in the glass says you're only a bum
If you can't look him straight in the eye.
You can fool the whole world down the pathway of years,
And get pats on the back as you pass,
But your final reward will be heartaches and tears
If you've cheated the guy in the glass.

Are you friends with the guy (or gal) in the glass? What will it take to be at peace with that person?

"To be yourself in a world that is constantly trying to make you something else is the greatest accomplishment."
- Ralph Waldo Emerson

Character is destiny.

Character is destiny. This is true for a person, a marriage, a family, and yes, for a nation. What does our future look like if that is true? Maybe it's time to place character back at the center of our families, communities, and education system. Whatever it is we wish to rebuild in our lives and in our nation, let us begin with character.

How do you build character? With virtue. Virtues are the building blocks of character. Think about this short list of virtues: patience, kindness, humility, gentleness, perseverance, truthfulness, courage, temperance, justice, faithfulness, and goodwill. Would your life improve if you had more of these virtues, in both number and degree? Would you be a better spouse? Would you be a better parent? A better sibling, friend, colleague, neighbor, and citizen?

People of exceptional character put character first. They put it above everything else. It doesn't matter what it costs them, because they know that to abandon character would be to lose their very self.

How would your life be different if you put character at the center?

"Character cannot be developed in ease and quiet. Only through experience of trial and suffering can the soul be strengthened, ambition inspired, and success achieved." - Helen Keller

Alignment issues.

Stress, unhappiness, anxiety, and depression are not bad things. They are not human malfunctions. Quite the opposite, they are proof that everything is working as it should. They come to us as messengers, to tap us on the shoulder and point out that our lives have slipped out of alignment.

We are most fully human, and most fully alive, when we are living an integrated life. This is integrity: aligning our actions with what we know to be good, true, just, and right.

When we turn our backs on what is good, true, just, and right, when we abandon our highest values, our integrity gets eroded. This always results in a loss of self, great or small. When our integrity is being eroded, you can be sure a number of other things are happening too. We are losing sight of who we are and what we value. We are losing our sense of self, which leads to an identity crisis. But all along the way, we are hurting people, often the people we claim to love the most, and always ourselves.

Misalignment always leads to pain and suffering for you and for others. What area of your life is misaligned? It takes boldness to admit it. How do you realign your life and live with more integrity than ever before? One decision at a time. Move your heart and mind into agreement, and act out of that united self.

What area of your life is misaligned?

"Happiness is when what you think, what you say, and what you do are in harmony." - Mahatma Gandhi

Measuring your life.

What measuring stick do you use to assess your life? Career? Money? Status? Stuff? Education? Popularity? Integrity? Happiness? Adventure? Health?

At different points in our lives, we all use some of these to measure our lives, but over time most of us move on to things that are harder to measure. How many people love you? Do you love what you do? Do you feel like you are doing what you were born to do? How many other people have you helped to become successful, happy, educated? How many lives have you improved? How long will you be remembered after you die? Are you at peace with God?

These are enormous questions, but we should not let that intimidate us. How do you measure your life? What do you look for when deciding if you are on the right path? How do you judge your progress?

How do you measure your life?

"I have learned that success is to be measured not so much by the position that one has reached in life as by the obstacles which he has had to overcome while trying to succeed." - Booker T. Washington

Remember.

It's important to remember your story. You have been through tough times before and you weathered the storm. You have had many wonderful experiences in life. You have so much to be grateful for. But we forget.

A person who forgets his or her story goes mad. Couples who forget their stories become impatient and grow apart. Parents and children who forget their story lose their tenderness. And a society that forgets its story is doomed to make the same mistakes all over again. Take time to remember.

What is your story?

"Gratitude is the memory of the heart." - Saint Mary Euphrasia

Peace, serenity, and tranquility.

Some words are angry, others are harsh, some are firm, others are weak or neutral. These three words are beautiful: peace, serenity, and tranquility. Say them quietly aloud, over and over, for two minutes. Take note of how these words make you feel. You will be amazed how just saying these beautiful words invites them into the depths of your being. Invite peace, serenity, and tranquility into your life.

Think about a time in your life where you experienced peace, serenity, and tranquility. What was different?

"Peace is the simplicity of heart, serenity of mind, tranquility of soul, the bond of love." - Padre Pio

The central question.

Life's biggest questions need to be personalized to a particular person. What's the meaning of life? is a question that has been pondered by lovers of wisdom for thousands of years. But the question that really matters to you is: What is the meaning of *your* life?

What is the meaning of *your* life?

"For the meaning of life differs from man to man, from day to day and from hour to hour. What matters, therefore, is not the meaning of life in general but rather the specific meaning of a person's life at a given moment." - Victor Frankl

The mountaintop.

Death comes to us all. When death approaches, the person you have become meets the person you could have been. This is a humbling encounter. Don't wait for it. Meet with the person you are capable of becoming for a few minutes each day. The more time you spend in these meetings the less you will fear death. Use your thoughts, words, choices, and actions, to close the gap between who you are today and who you are capable of being. This is the path that leads to a deeply fulfilling life.

Who is the person you are capable of becoming?

"Continuous effort—not strength or intelligence—is the key to unlocking our potential." - Winston Churchill

The good life.

There is no secret to the good life. It isn't a mystery. No exceptional talent is required. It isn't only for the rich and famous. It is available to everyone, everywhere, at all times What is the essential ingredient of the good life? Goodness itself. The secret to the so-called good life has always been right before our very eyes. If you wish to live the good life, fill your life with goodness. Fill your life with love, kindness, gratitude, compassion, and generosity.

Take risks with your goodness. Test the limits of your goodness. Don't just love, astonish people with your love. Don't just dabble in generosity, live a life of staggering generosity.

How would your life change if your only goal was to do as much good as possible? Let's find out. Don't let this question remain unanswered. Celebrate goodness every chance you get.

Don't waste your gold dust.

How would your life change if your only goal was to do as much good as possible?

"Although the life of a person is in a land full of thorns and weeds, there is always a space in which the good seed can grow. You have to trust God." - Pope Francis